ABC Letters • Handwriting Practice • Phonic Match

ALPHABET TRACE PRACTICE

PRESCHOOL ACTIVITY BOOK

Missing Letters • Vocabulary • Missing sounds

Matching Letters • Alphabetical Order

ALPHABET LETTERS

A IS FOR... **APPLE**

B IS FOR... **BOOK**

C IS FOR... **CAR**

D IS FOR... **DOPHIN**

E IS FOR... **EMAIL**

F IS FOR... **FROG**

G IS FOR... **GRAPES**

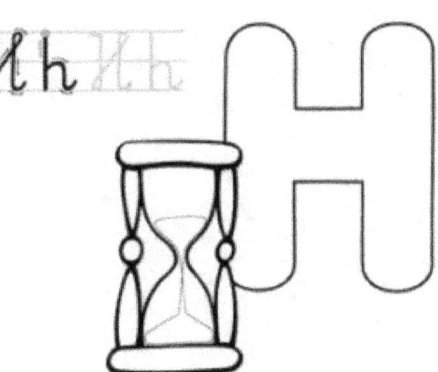

H IS FOR... **HOURGLASS**

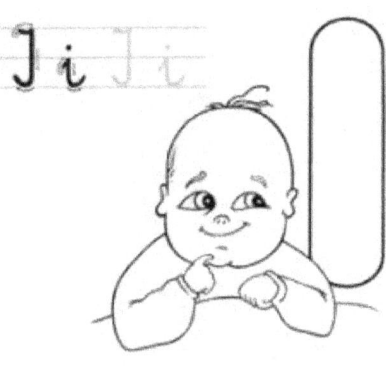

I IS FOR... **INFANT**

ALPHABET LETTERS

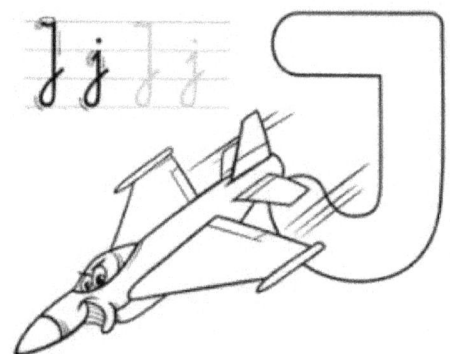
J IS FOR... **JET**

K IS FOR... **KIWI**

L IS FOR... **LADDER**

M IS FOR... **MACAW**

N IS FOR... **NEWSPAPER**

O IS FOR... **ORANGE**

P IS FOR... **PIRATE**

Q IS FOR... **QUADRUPLETS**

R IS FOR... **RHINOCEROS**

ALPHABET LETTERS

S IS FOR... **SEAHORSE**

T IS FOR... **TEDDY BEAR**

U IS FOR... **UNIFORM**

V IS FOR... **VAMPIRE**

W IS FOR... **WATERMELON**

X IS FOR... **X-RAY FISH**

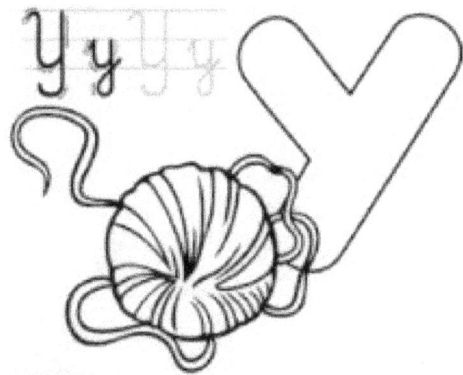

Y IS FOR... **YARN**

Z IS FOR... **ZERO**

Draw the Way

Tracing Practice

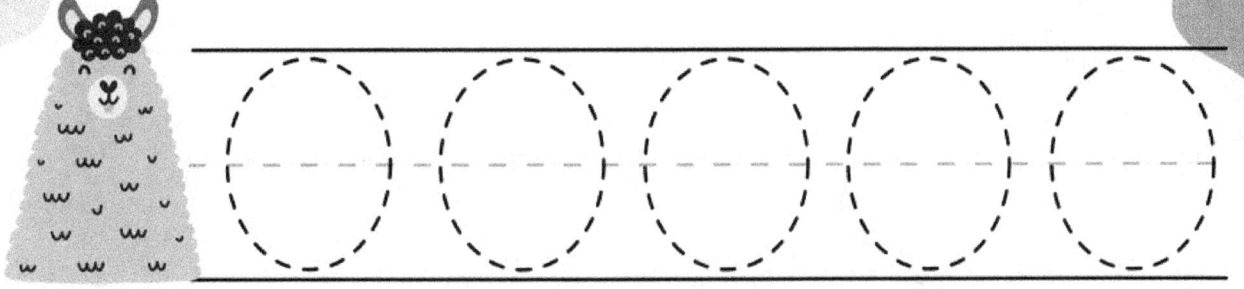

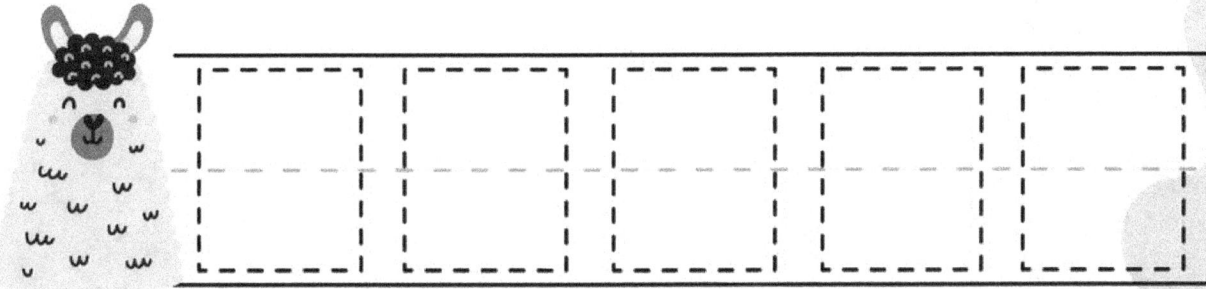

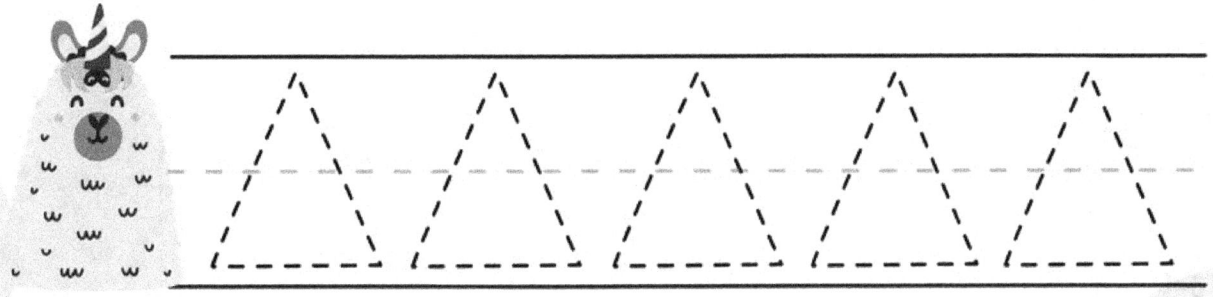

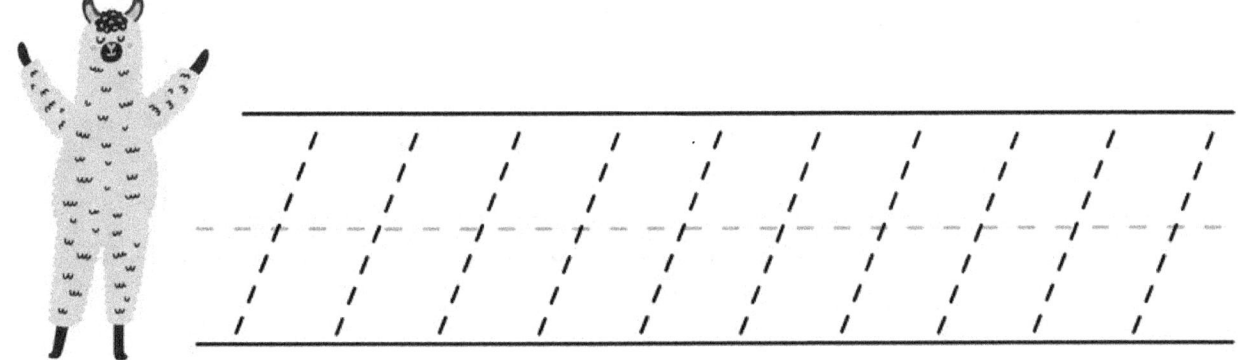

Tracing Practice

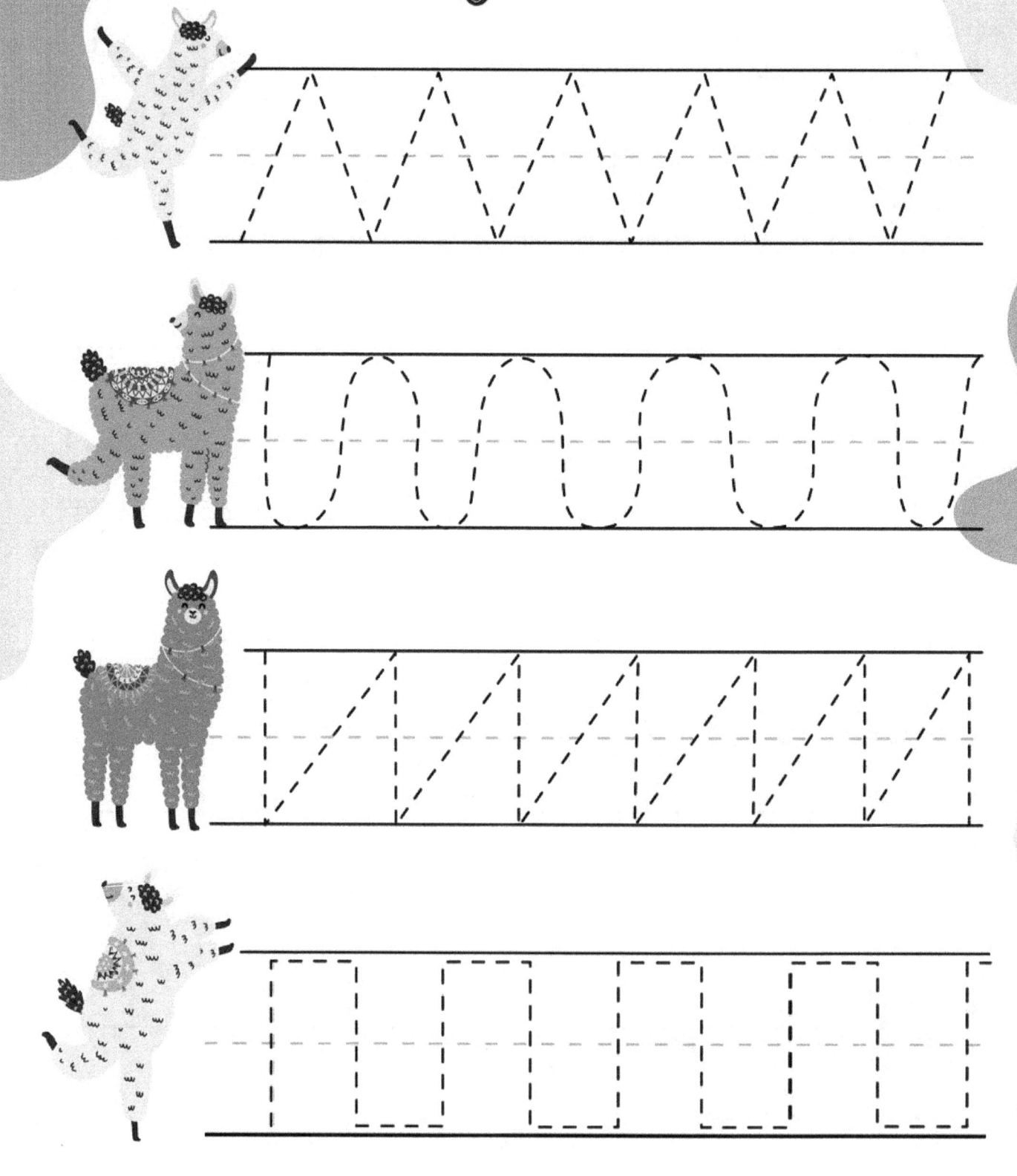

TRACE THE LINES

Connect the letter with the picture

F

G

H

I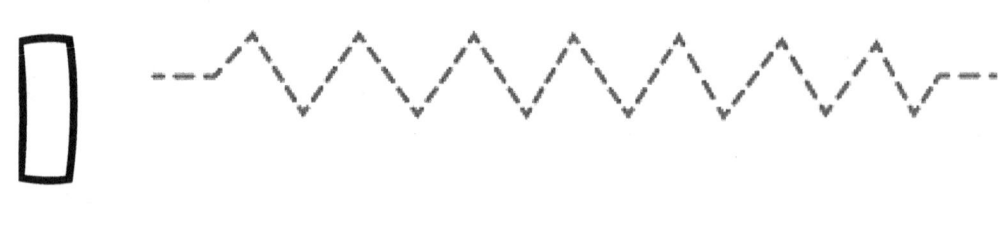

J

TRACE THE LINES

Connect the letter with the picture

P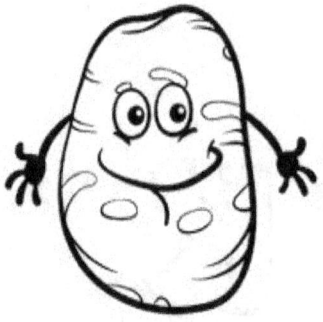

Q

R

S

T

TRACE THE LINES

Connect the letter with the picture

U

V

W

X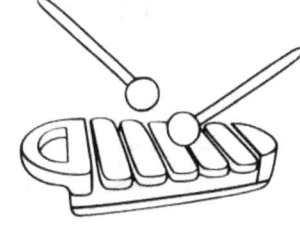

Y

Z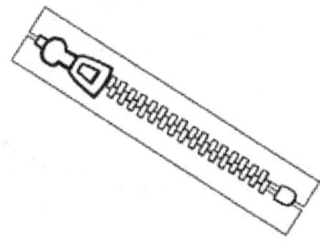

A a A a

A A A A A A A A A
A A A A A A A A A
A A A A A

a a a a a a a a a
a a a a a a a a a
a a a a a

Astronaut
Apple

B

Bb Bb

B B B B B B B B B B

B B B B B B B B B B

B B B B B

b b b b b b b b b b

b b b b b b b b b b

b b b b b

Book

broccoli

Dd Dd

D D D D D D D D D D D
D D D D D D D D D D D
D D D D D D

d d d d d d d d d d
d d d d d d d d d d
d d d d d

Dog dog
dinosaur

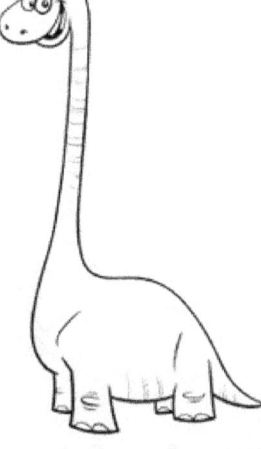

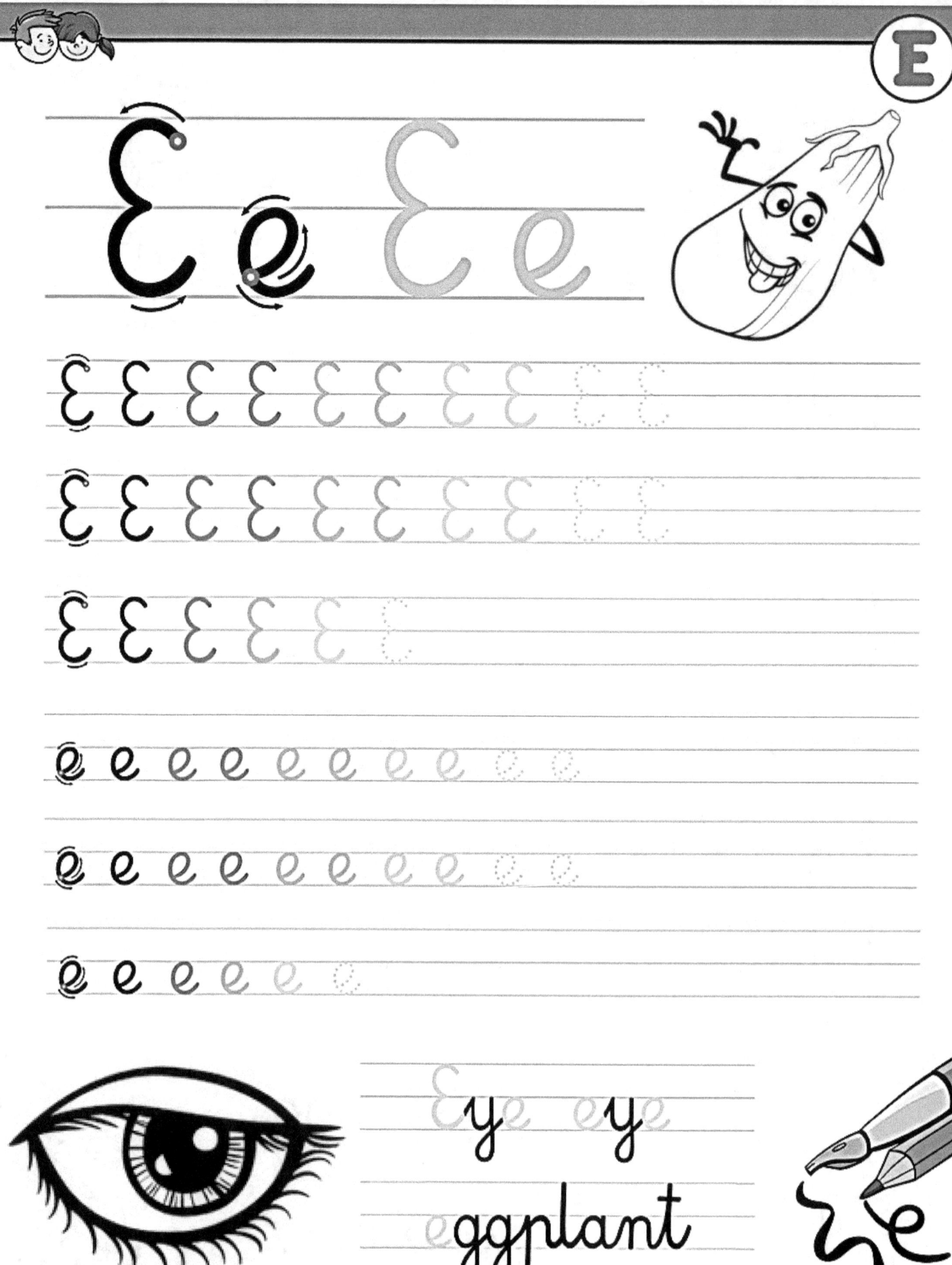

eye
eggplant

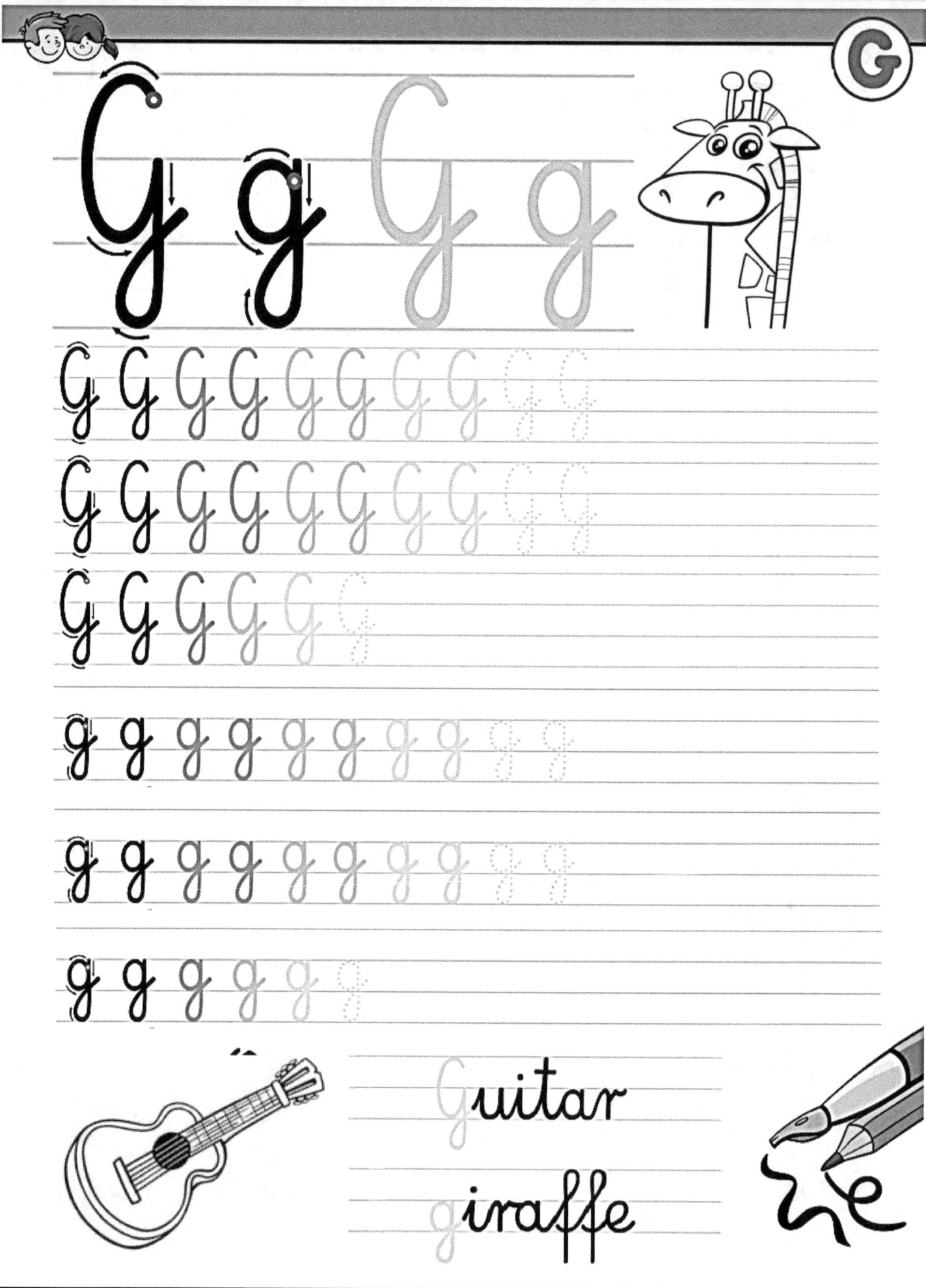

J i J i

J J J J J J J J

J J J J J J J J

J J J J J

i i i i i i i i i

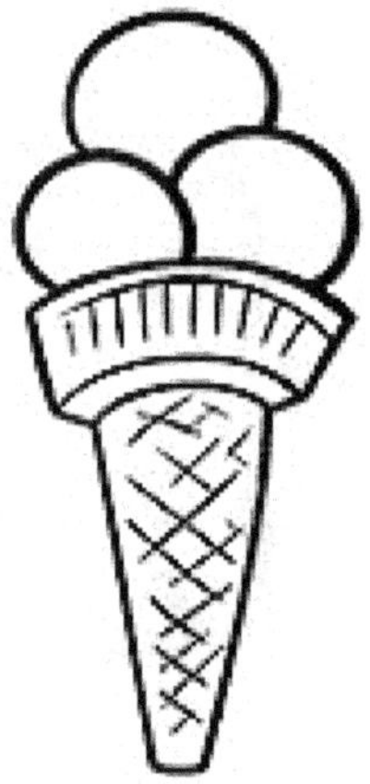

i i i i i i i i

i i i i i

Iguana

ice cream

K k

K K K K K K K K K

K K K K K K K K K

K K K K K

k k k k k k k

k k k k k k k

k k k k k

Kangaroo

koala

Mm Mm

M M M M M M

M M M M M M

M M M M

m m m m m m

m m m m m m

m m m m

Monkey

melon

Nn Nn

N N N N N N N N N N

N N N N N N N N N N

N N N N N N

n n n n n n n n

n n n n n n n n

n n n n n n

Nine

newspaper

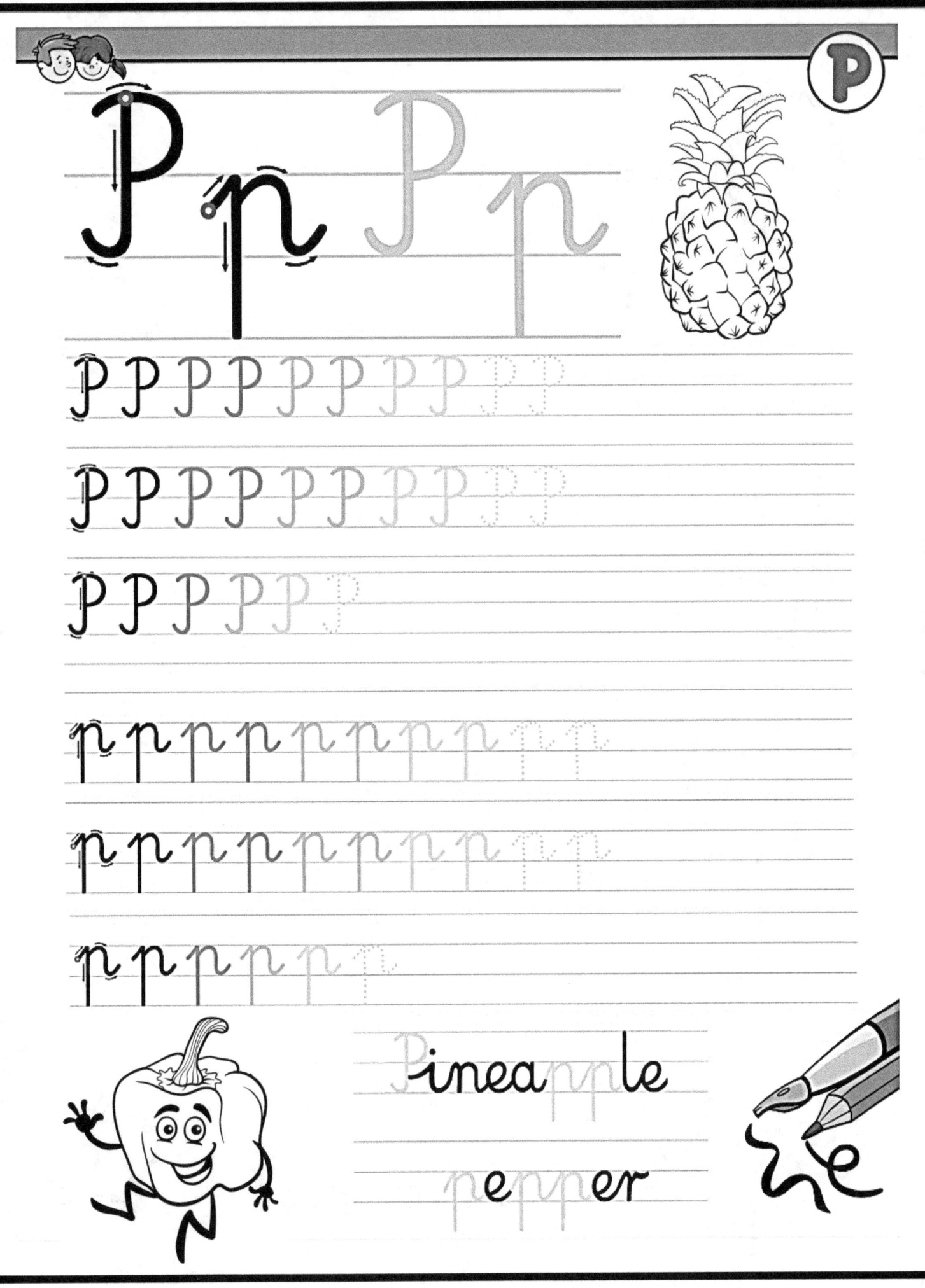

T

T t T t

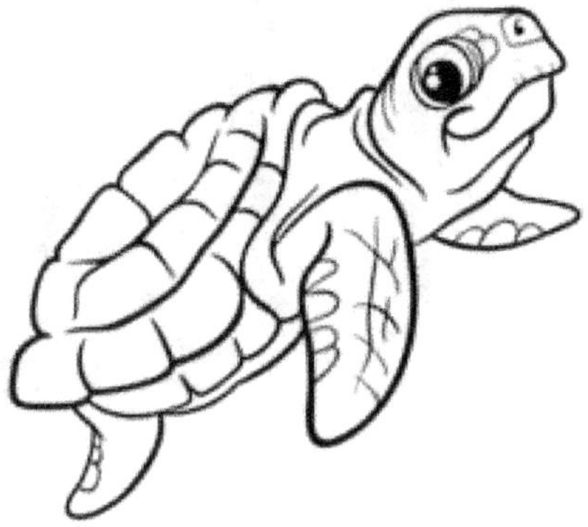

T T T T T T T T T T

T T T T T T T T T T

T T T T T T

t t t t t t t t t t

t t t t t t t t t t

t t t t t t

Turtle

tractor

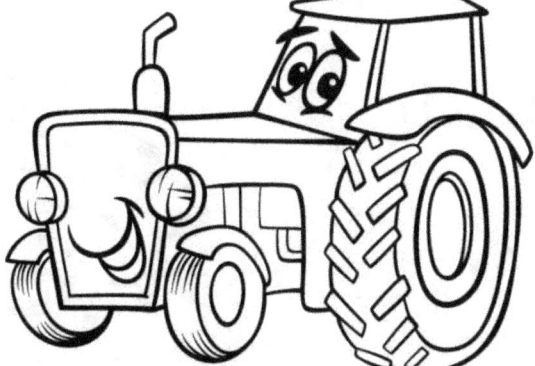

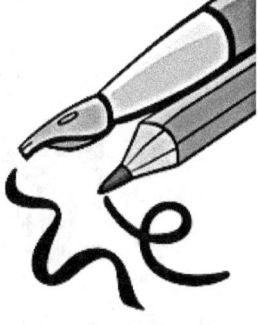

Uu

Uu Uu

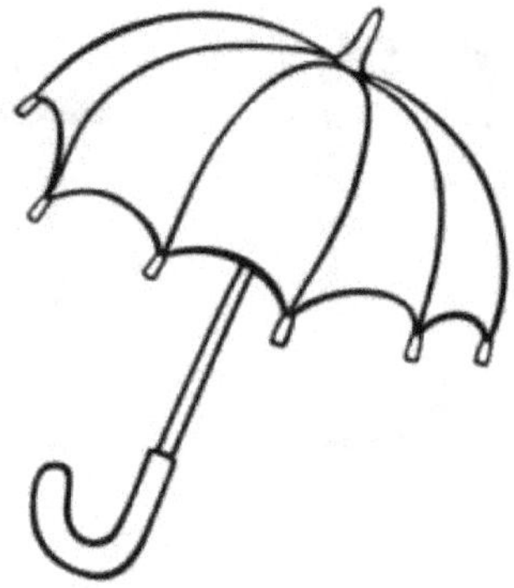

U U U U U U U U

U U U U U U U U

U U U U U

u u u u u u u

u u u u u u u

u u u u u

Umbrella

uniform

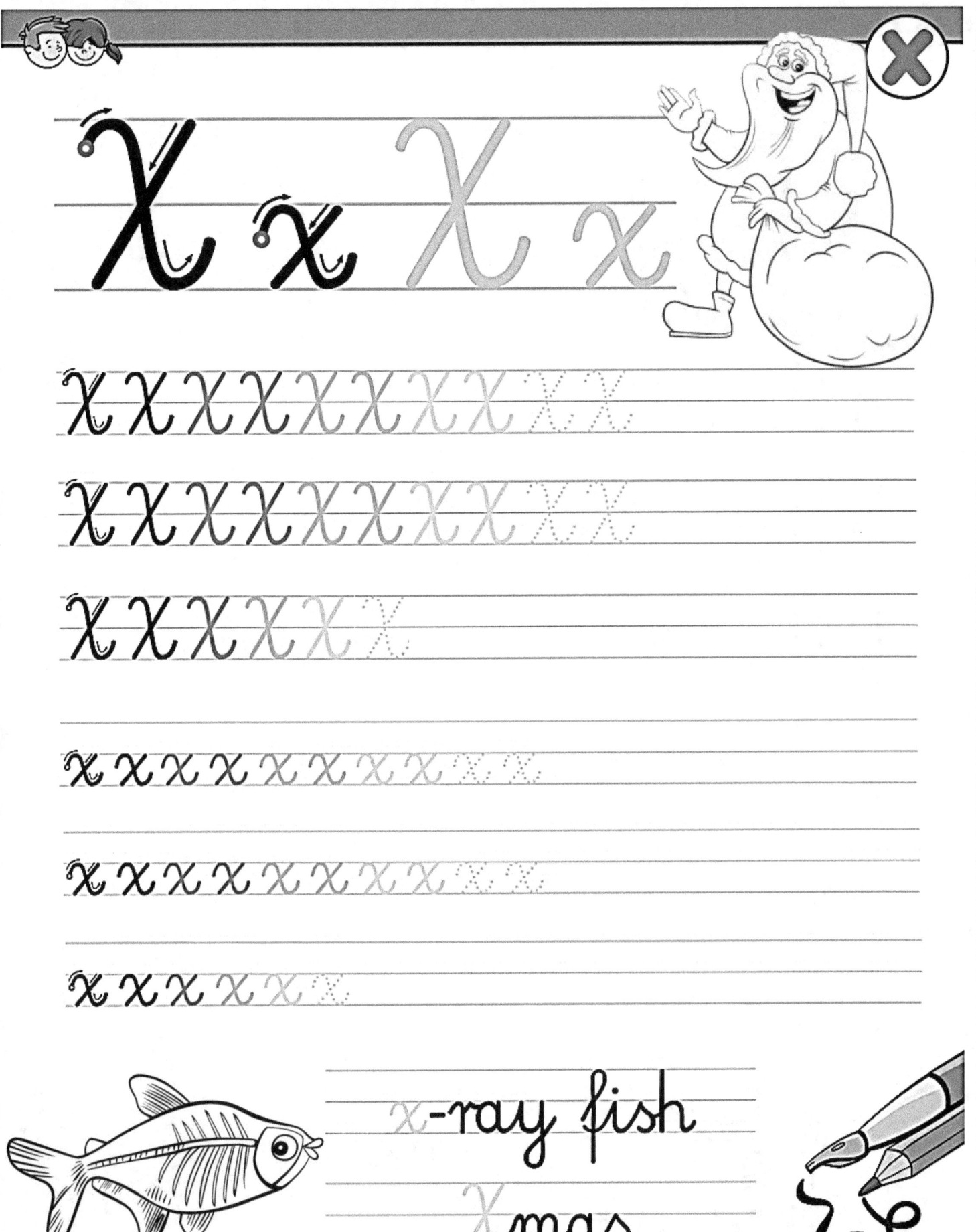

Z

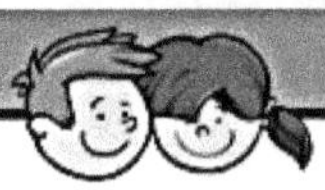

Zz Zz

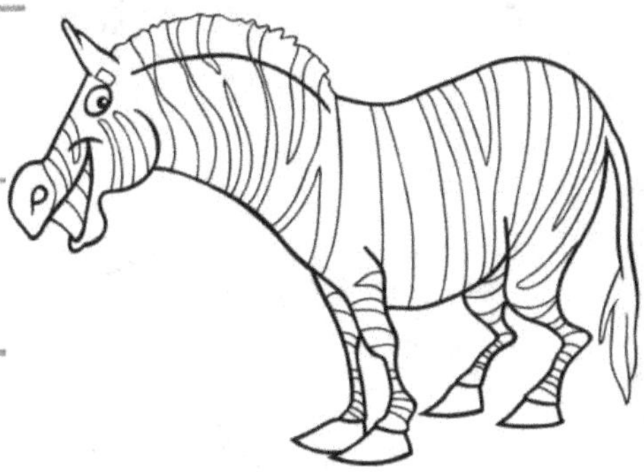

Z Z Z Z Z Z Z Z Z Z

Z Z Z Z Z Z Z Z Z Z

Z Z Z Z Z Z

z z z z z z z z z z

z z z z z z z z z z

z z z z z z

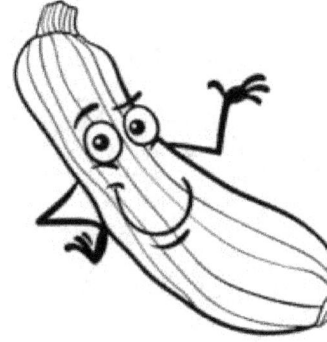

Zebra

zucchini

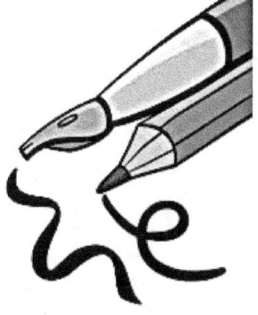

PHONIC MATCH

Draw a line from the letter "A" to the pictures that begin with A/a sound.

Read the letter and say the pictures aloud

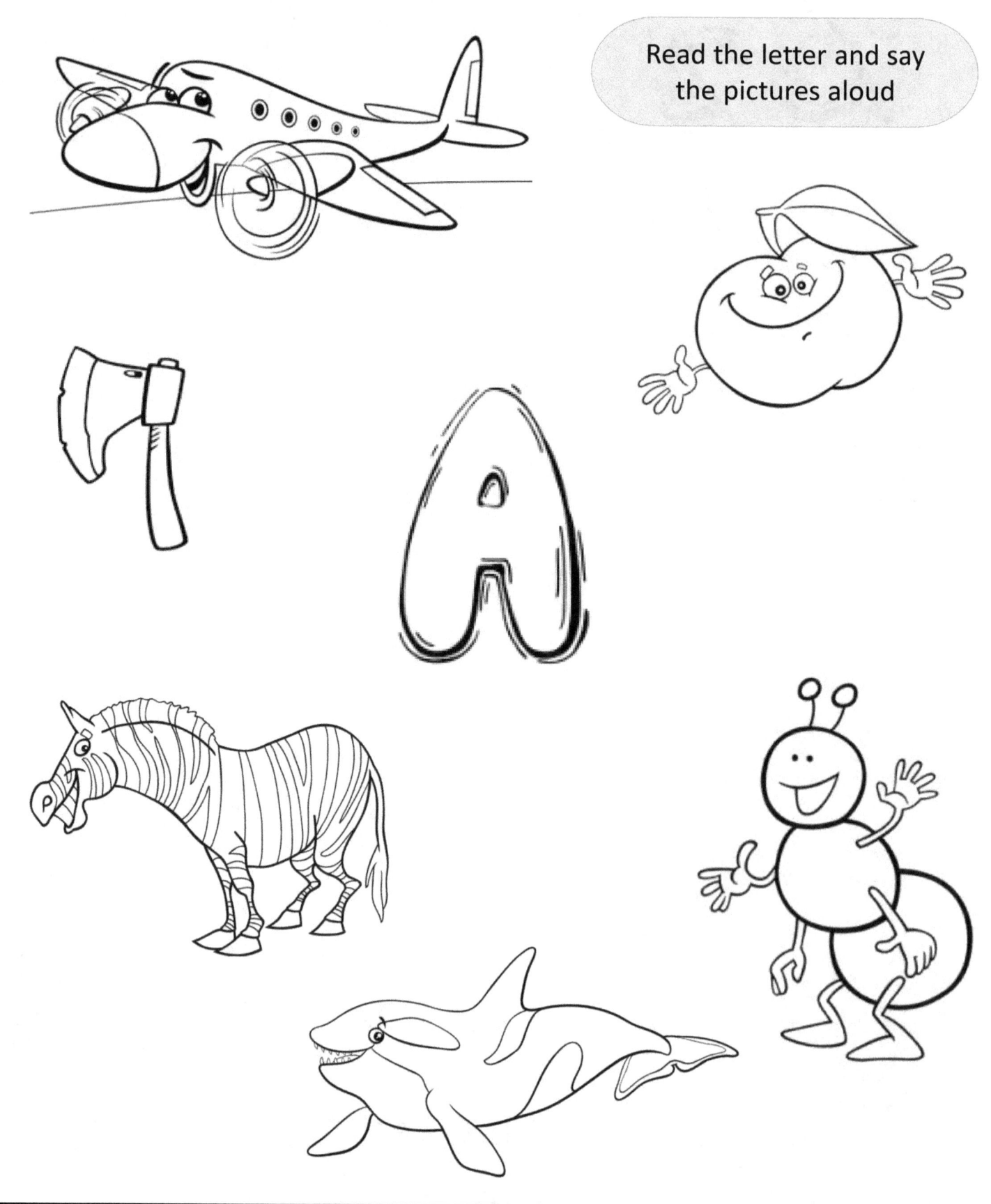

PHONIC MATCH

Draw a line from the letter "B" to the pictures that begin with **B/b** sound.

Read the letter and say the pictures aloud

PHONIC MATCH

Draw a line from the letter "C" to the pictures that begin with C/c sound.

Read the letter and say the pictures aloud

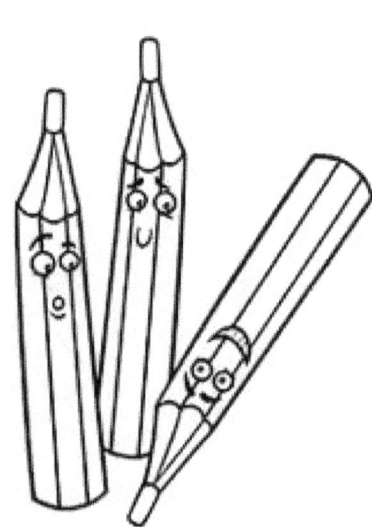  

PHONIC MATCH

Draw a line from the letter "D" to the pictures that begin with D/d sound.

Read the letter and say the pictures aloud

PHONIC MATCH

Draw a line from the letter "E" to the pictures that begin with **E/e** sound.

> Read the letter and say the pictures aloud

PHONIC MATCH

Draw a line from the letter "F" to the pictures that begin with **F/f** sound.

Read the letter and say the pictures aloud

PHONIC MATCH

Draw a line from the letter "G" to the pictures that begin with **G/g** sound.

Read the letter and say the pictures aloud

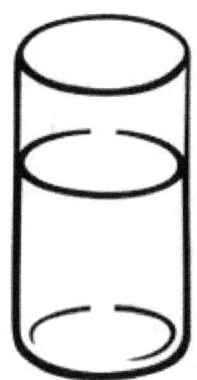

PHONIC MATCH

Draw a line from the letter "H" to the pictures that begin with H/h sound.

Read the letter and say the pictures aloud

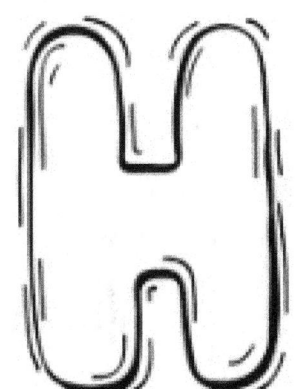

PHONIC MATCH

Draw a line from the letter "I" to the pictures that begin with I/i sound.

Read the letter and say the pictures aloud

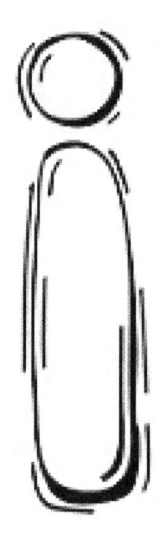

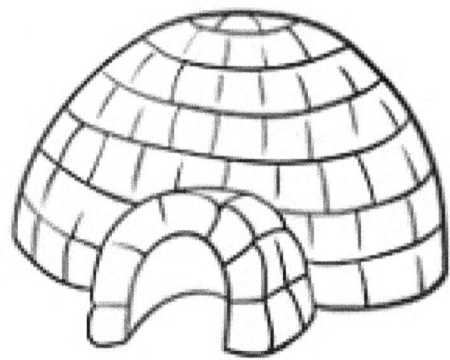

PHONIC MATCH

Draw a line from the letter "J" to the pictures that begin with **J/j** sound.

Read the letter and say the pictures aloud

PHONIC MATCH

Draw a line from the letter "**K**" to the pictures that begin with **K/k** sound.

Read the letter and say the pictures aloud

PHONIC MATCH

Draw a line from the letter "L" to the pictures that begin with L/l sound.

Read the letter and say the pictures aloud

PHONIC MATCH

Draw a line from the letter "M" to the pictures that begin with M/m sound.

Read the letter and say the pictures aloud

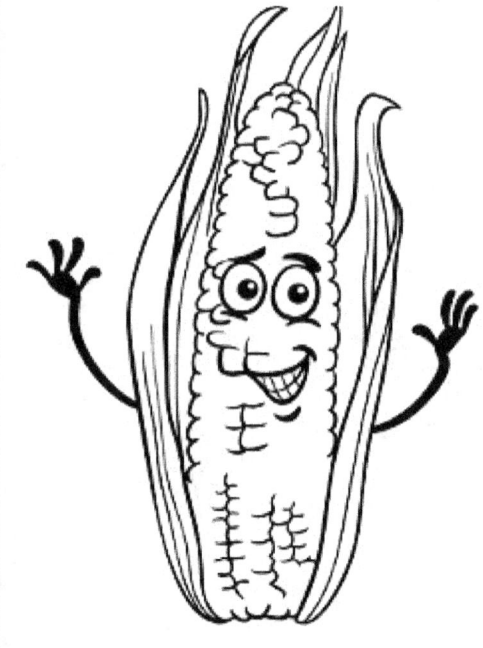

PHONIC MATCH

Draw a line from the letter "N" to the pictures that begin with **N/n** sound.

Read the letter and say the pictures aloud

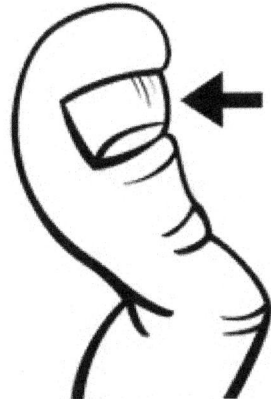

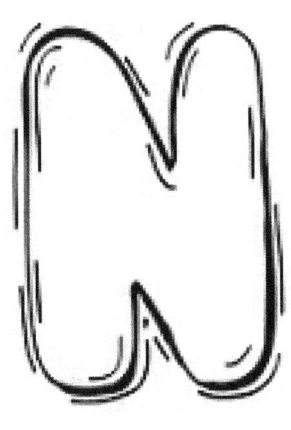

PHONIC MATCH

Draw a line from the letter "O" to the pictures that begin with **O/o** sound.

Read the letter and say the pictures aloud

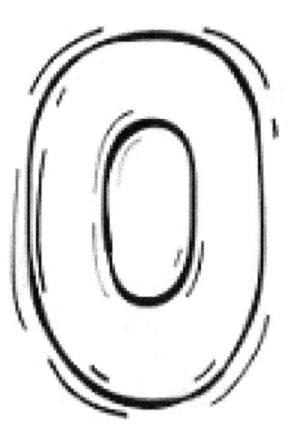

PHONIC MATCH

Draw a line from the letter "P" to the pictures that begin with **P/p** sound.

Read the letter and say the pictures aloud

PHONIC MATCH

Draw a line from the letter "Q" to the pictures that begin with Q/q sound.

Read the letter and say the pictures aloud

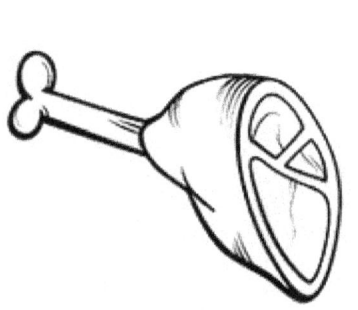

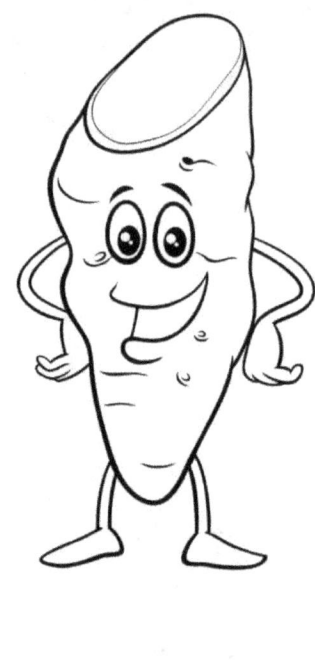

PHONIC MATCH

Draw a line from the letter "**R**" to the pictures that begin with **R/r** sound.

Read the letter and say the pictures aloud

PHONIC MATCH

Draw a line from the letter "S" to the pictures that begin with S/s sound.

Read the letter and say the pictures aloud

PHONIC MATCH

Draw a line from the letter "U" to the pictures that begin with U/u sound.

Read the letter and say the pictures aloud

PHONIC MATCH

Draw a line from the letter "V" to the pictures that begin with V/v sound.

Read the letter and say the pictures aloud

PHONIC MATCH

Draw a line from the letter "W" to the pictures that begin with **W/w** sound.

Read the letter and say the pictures aloud

PHONIC MATCH

Draw a line from the letter "**X**" to the pictures that begin with **X/x** sound.

Read the letter and say the pictures aloud

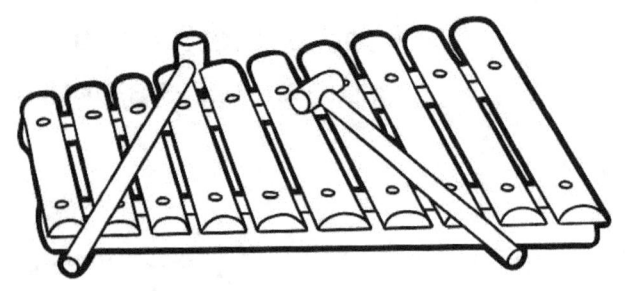

PHONIC MATCH

Draw a line from the letter "Y" to the pictures that begin with Y/y sound.

Read the letter and say the pictures aloud

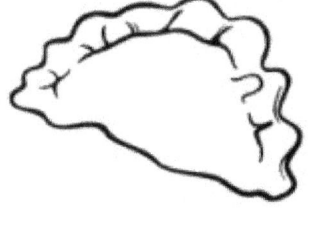

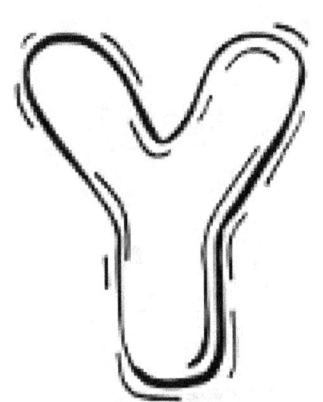

PHONIC MATCH

Draw a line from the letter "Z" to the pictures that begin with Z/z sound.

Read the letter and say the pictures aloud

MATCH THE LETTERS

Draw lines connecting each balloon to the child wearing the shirt with the matching letter.

MATCH THE LETTERS

Draw lines connecting each bee to the flower with the matching letter.

MATCH THE LETTERS

Draw lines connecting each leaf to the tree with the matching letter.

MATCH THE LETTERS

Draw lines connecting each teddy bear to the hat with the matching letter.

FIND THE LETTERS

Draw a circle around each letter in the word **bin**.

Draw a circle around each letter in the word **cup**.

FIND THE LETTERS

Draw a (circle) around each letter in the word **dog**.

Draw a (circle) around each letter in the word **hat**.

WRITE YOUR NAME

Find the first letter of your name in the box below and draw a (circle) around it. Then copy the letter onto the line at the bottom of the page. Now find the next letter. Keep going till you have written your name.

a b c d e f
g h i j k l
m n o p q r
s t u v w x
y z

My name is _____

UPPERCASE ALPHABET IN COLOR

Have fun coloring in each uppercase letter with a different color of your choice. For extra fun, outline each letter with multiple different colors to create a rainbow effect!

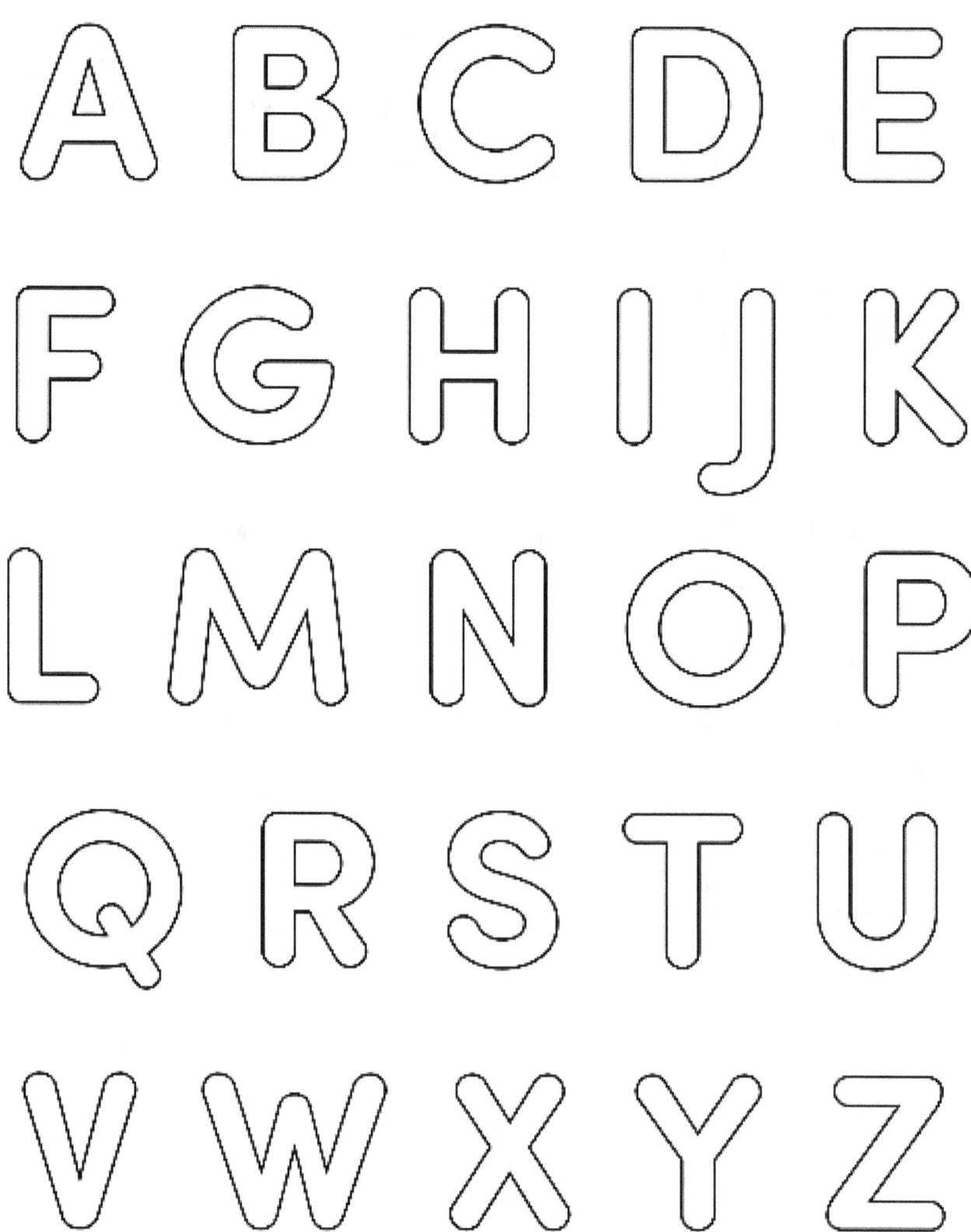

TRACE AND READ – UPPERCASE LETTERS

Trace and read the word

 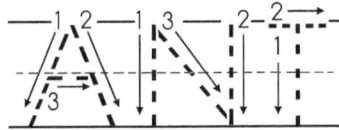 

 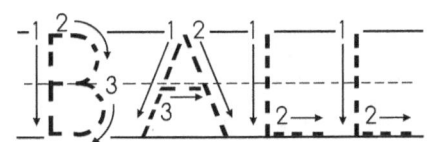

 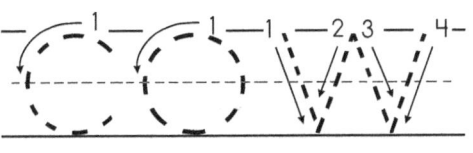

 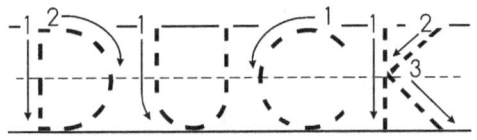

TRACE AND READ — UPPERCASE LETTERS

Trace and read the word

 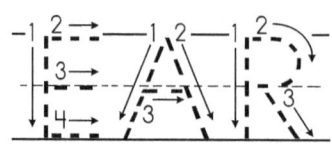 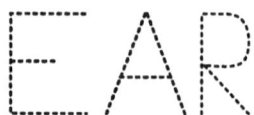

 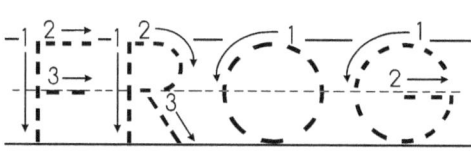

 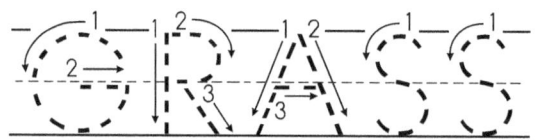

 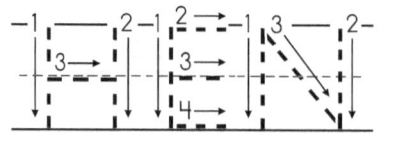 

 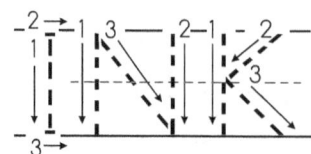

TRACE AND READ – UPPERCASE LETTERS

Trace and read the word

  JET

 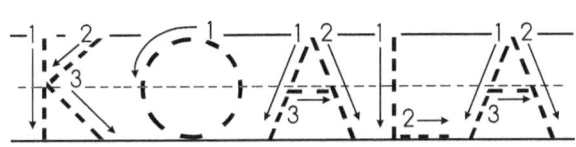

 KOALA

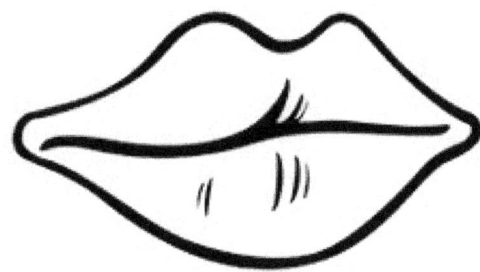 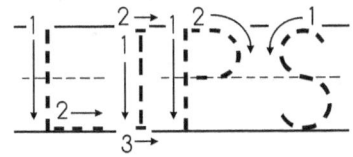  LIPS

 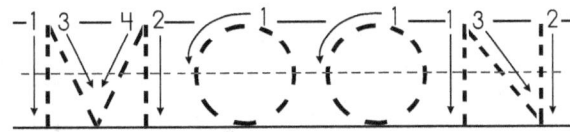

MOON

TRACE AND READ – UPPERCASE LETTERS

Trace and read the word

 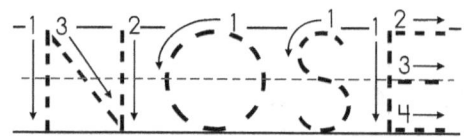 

 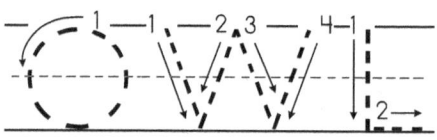 

 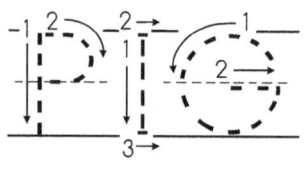 

 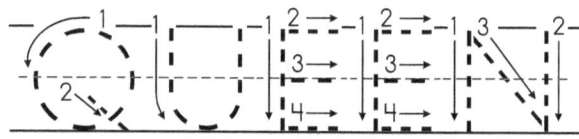

TRACE AND READ – UPPERCASE LETTERS

Trace and read the word

 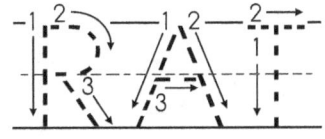 RAT

 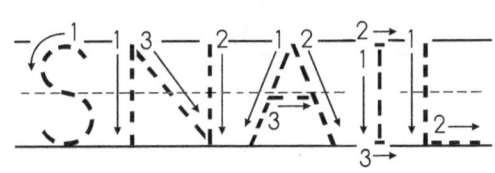 SNAIL

 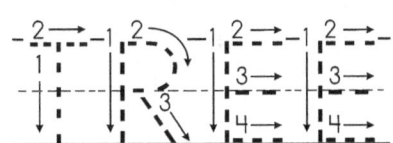 TREE

 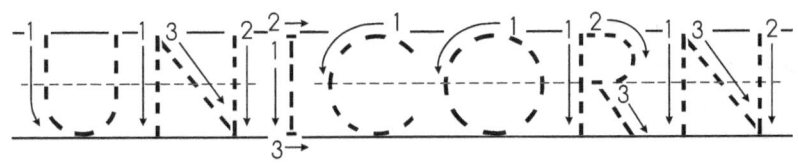

UNICORN

TRACE AND READ – UPPERCASE LETTERS

Trace and read the word

 VASE

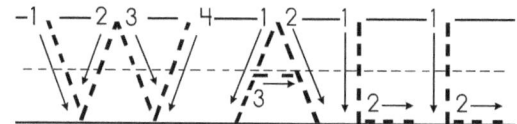 WALL

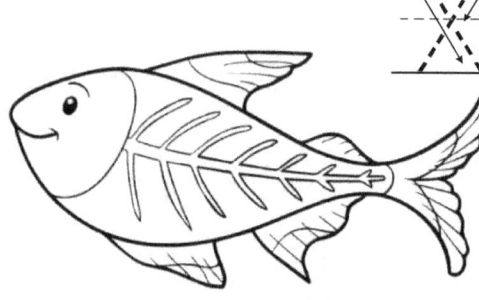

X-RAY FISH

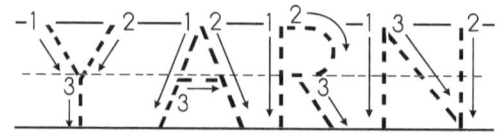 YARN

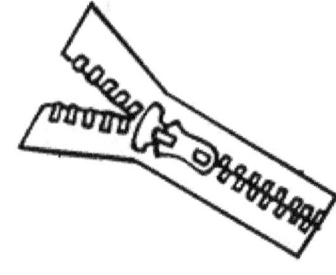
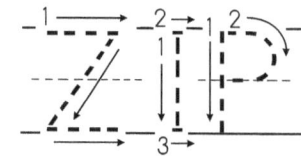 ZIP

LOWERCASE RAINBOW LETTERS

Trace each lowercase alphabet letter with a colored pencil. Trace each letter again with different pencil. Repeat several times to create a rainbow letters!

TRACE AND READ – LOWERCASE LETTERS

Trace and read the word

 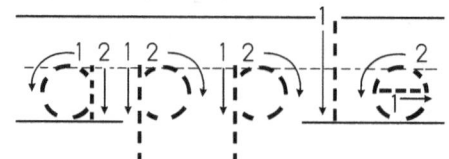 

 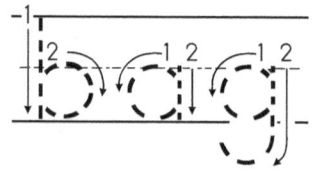 

 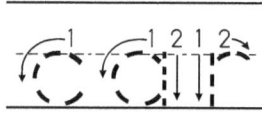 

 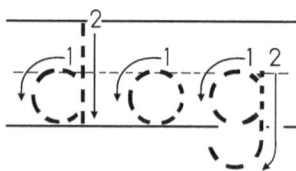 

 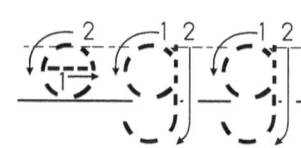 

TRACE AND READ – LOWERCASE LETTERS

Trace and read the word

 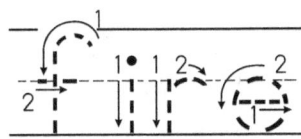 fire

 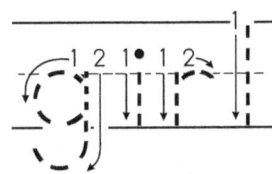 girl

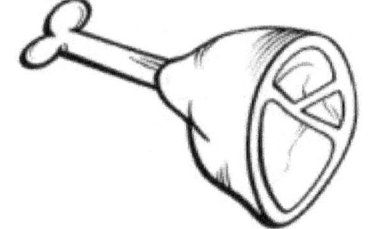 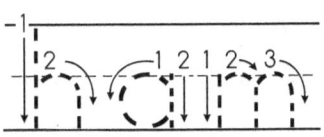 ham

 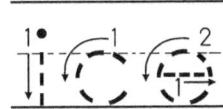 ice

 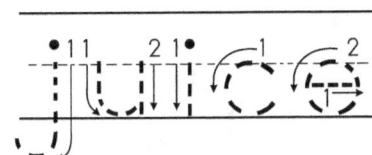 juice

TRACE AND READ – LOWERCASE LETTERS

Trace and read the word

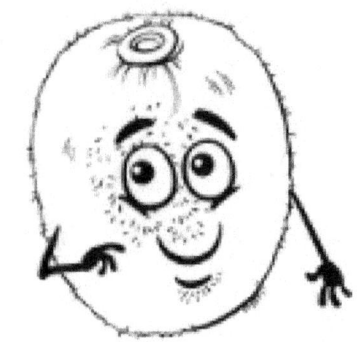 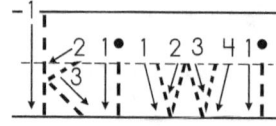  kiwi

 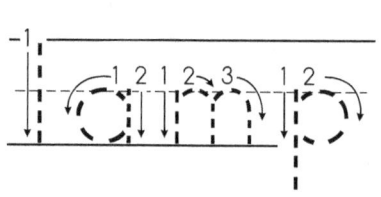  lamp

 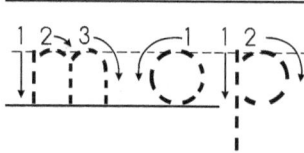  mop

  net

 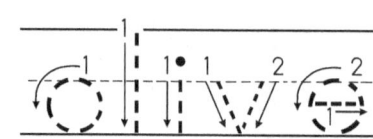 olive

TRACE AND READ – LOWERCASE LETTERS

Trace and read the word

 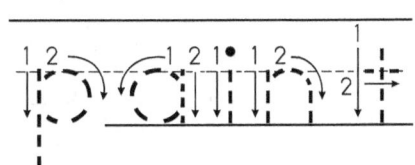 paint

 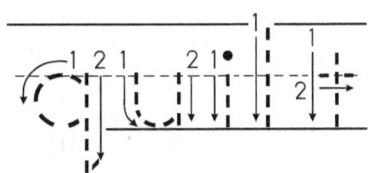 quilt

 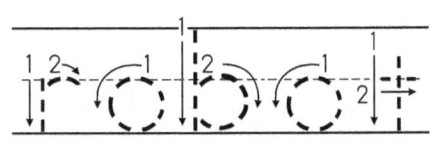 robot

 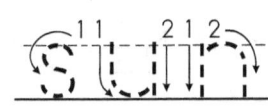 sun

TRACE AND READ – LOWERCASE LETTERS

Trace and read the word

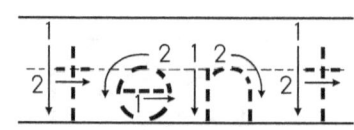 tent

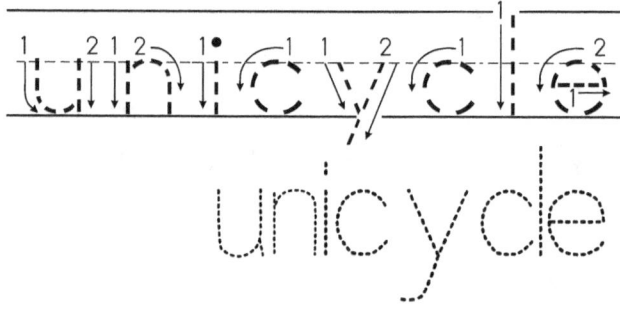
unicycle

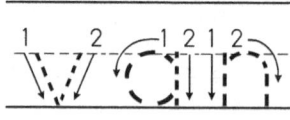 van

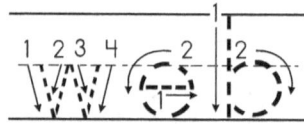 web

TRACE AND READ – LOWERCASE LETTERS

Trace and read the word

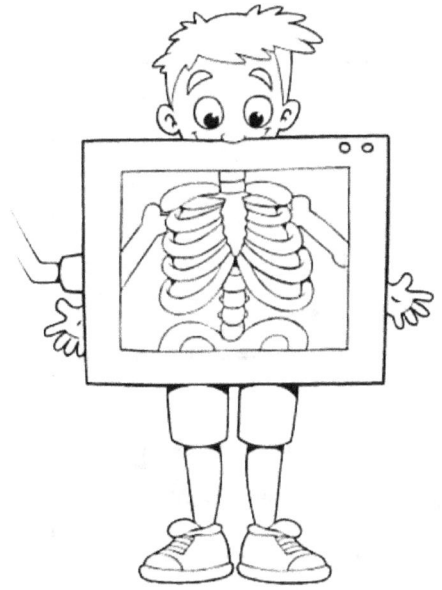
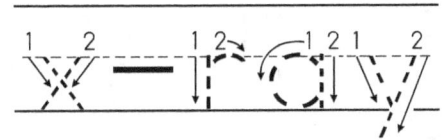

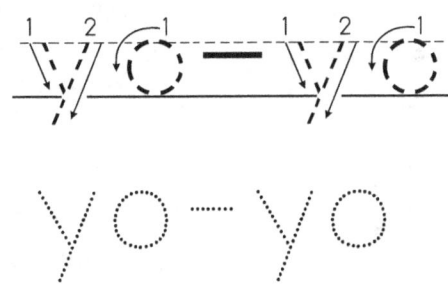

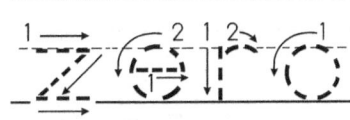

MISSING SOUND

Each word is missing a sound. Write the missing letter in the blank.

WHAT'S MY SOUND?

Shade the beginning sound of each picture

	c			s
	m			h
	u			t

	n			f
	a			c
	r			d

	e			a
	d			b
	b			x

	m			r
	b			w
	i			y

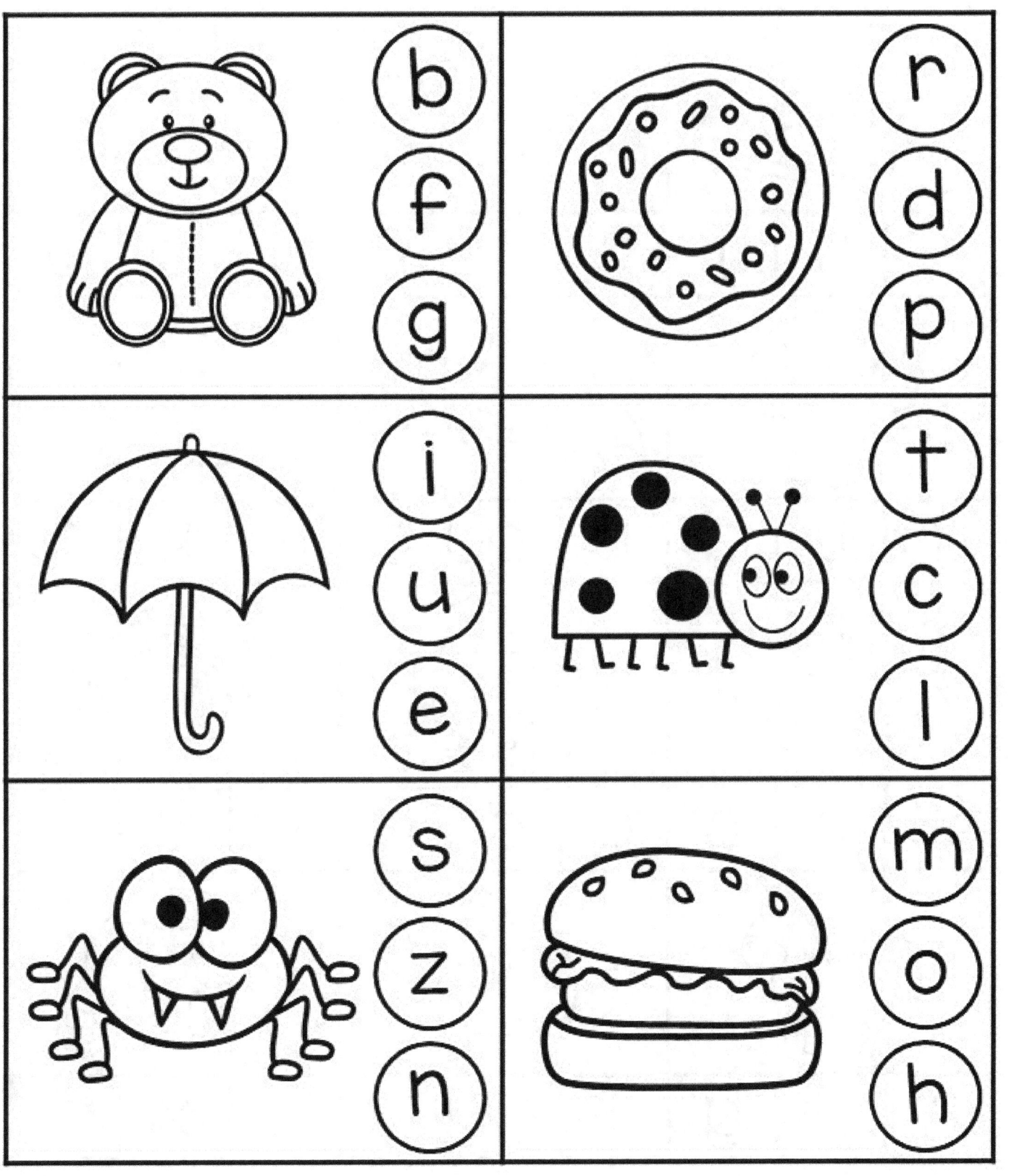

COLOR MY SOUND

Color the beginning sound of each picture.

| r | p | j | b | t | f | s | c | a |

| m | u | d | r | b | p | l | k | t |

| s | e | c | b | d | q | r | v | i |

| n | h | g | f | y | w | o | x | t |

WHAT'S IN THE MIDDLE?

Color the middle sound of each picture and write the missing letter.

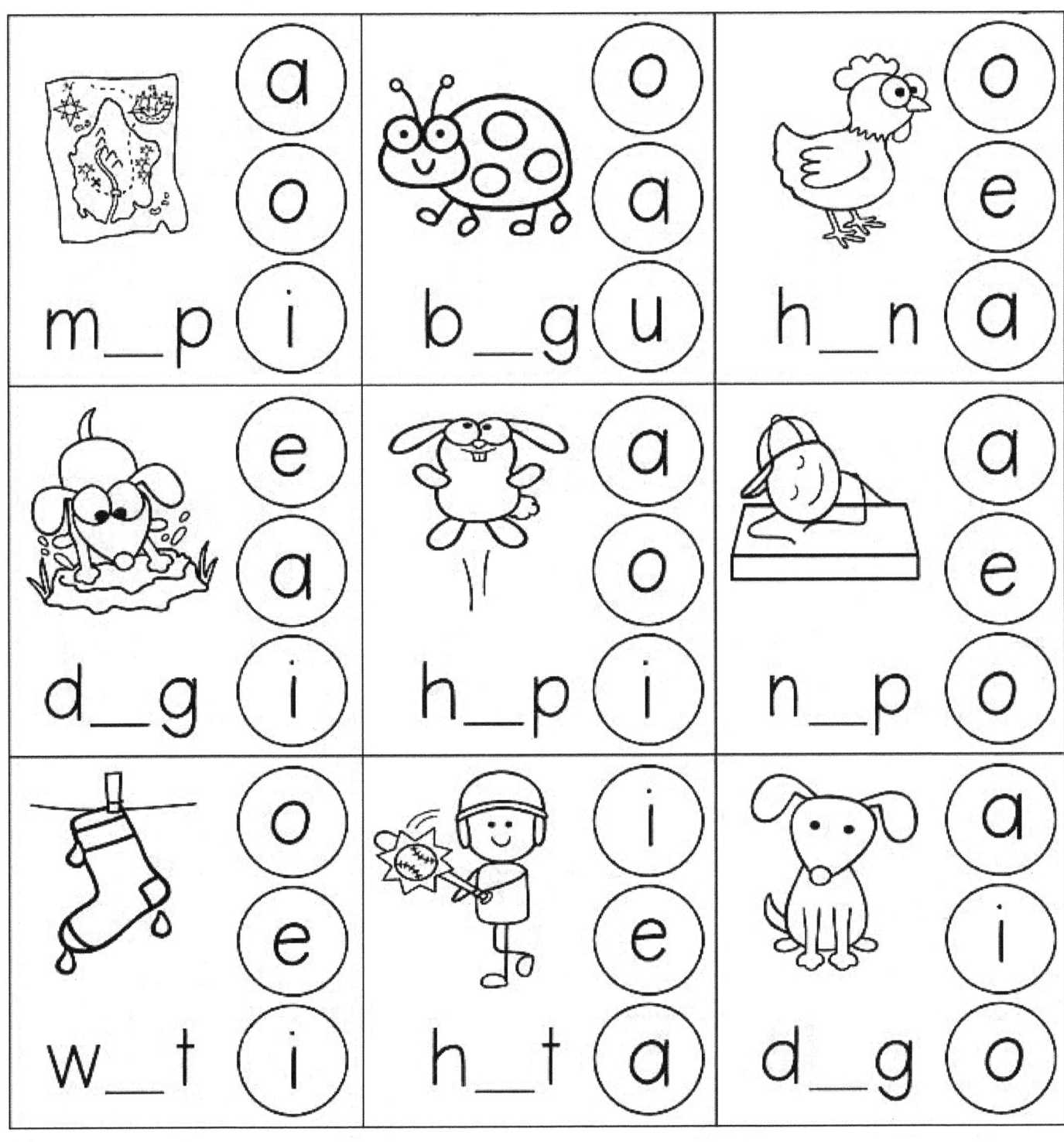

WHAT'S IN THE MIDDLE?

Write the middle sound of each picture.

 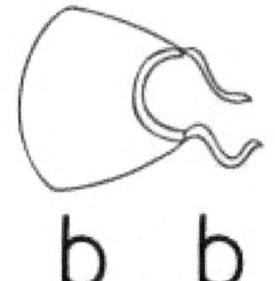 

l_g   b_b   w_b

 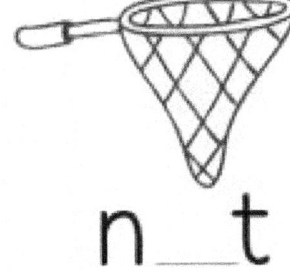 

s_n   n_t   b_t

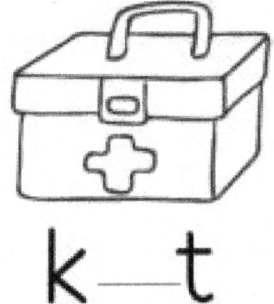 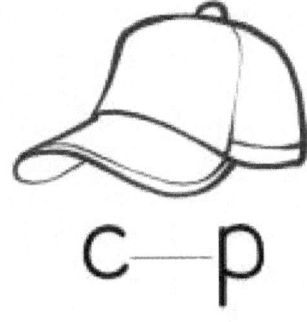 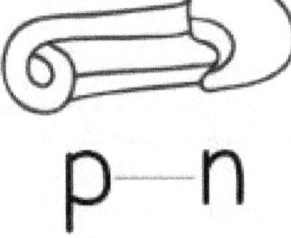

k_t   c_p   p_n

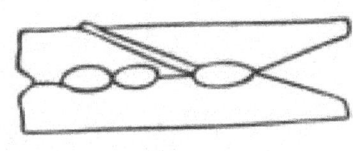  

p_g   b_s   m_g

WHAT'S IN THE MIDDLE?

Write the middle sound of each picture.

ENDING SOUNDS

Say the name of each picture. Circle the letter that represents the ending sound of the picture. Write the letter to complete the word.

l t

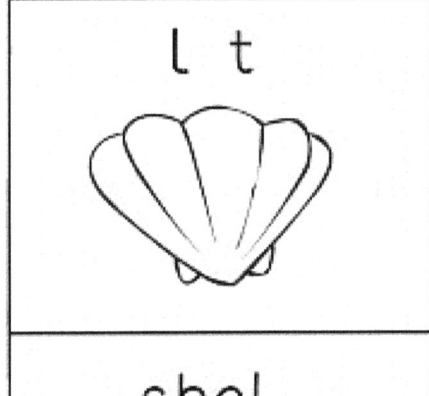

shel__

m t

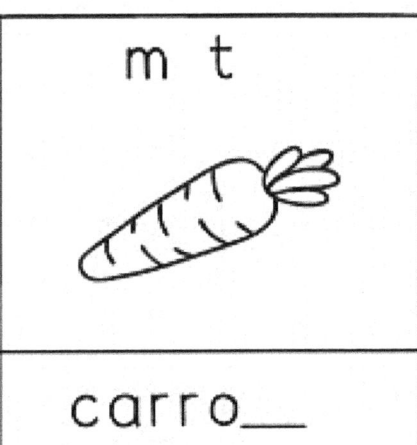

carro__

n h

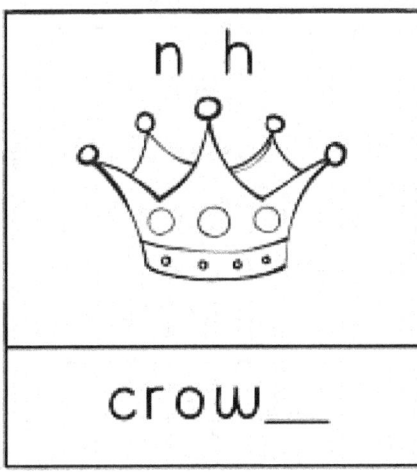

crow__

p q

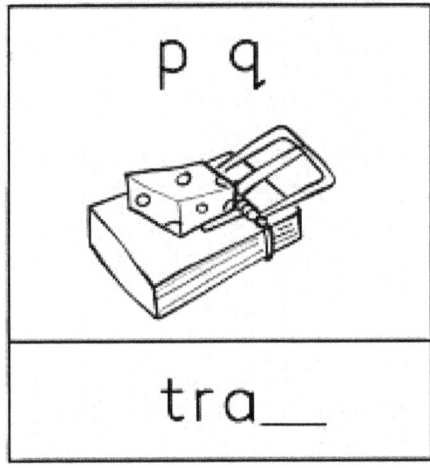

tra__

e s

bu__

f b

lea__

k g

fla__

w m

co__

s k

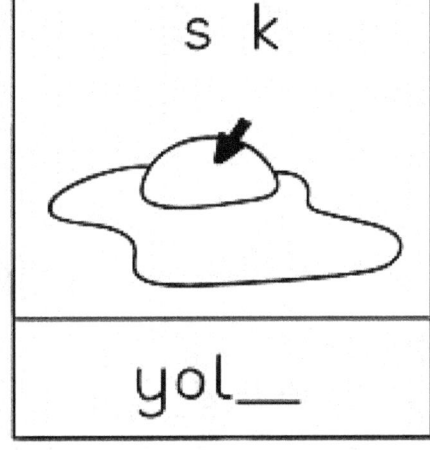

yol__

ENDING SOUNDS

Say the name of each picture. Circle the letter that represents the ending sound of the picture. Write the letter to complete the word.

o i  yoy__	x n  wago__	o a  banan__
u n  he__	t j 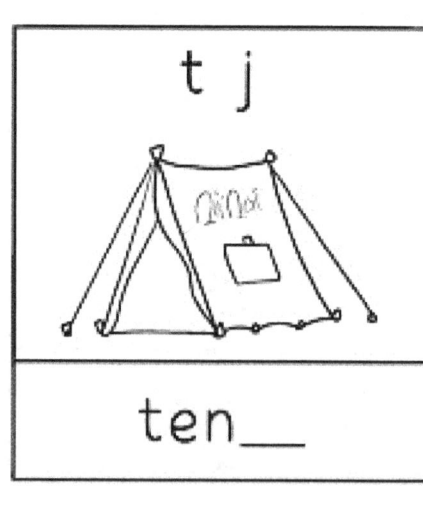 ten__	v p  shee __
k d 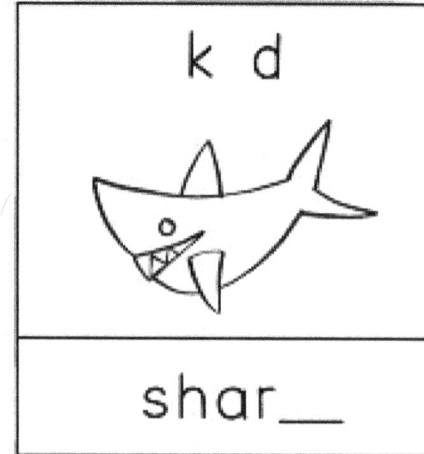 shar__	w r 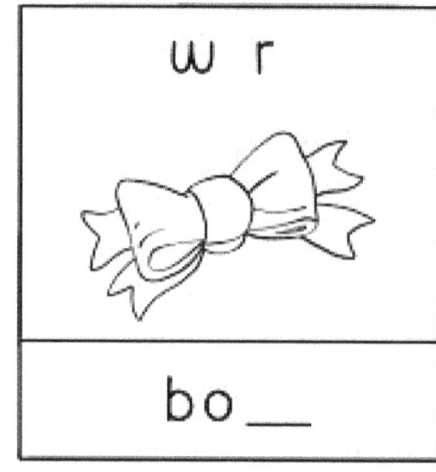 bo__	g n 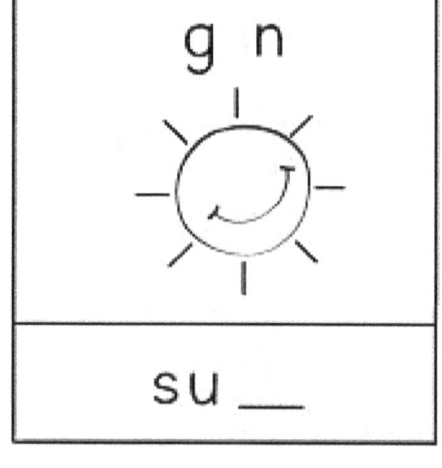 su __

ALPHABET UPPERCASE LETTERS

Write the uppercase letters

A   B   C   D
E   F   G   H
I   J   K   L
M   N   O   P
Q   R   S   T
U   V   W   X
      Y   Z

ALPHABET LOWERCASE LETTERS

Write the lowercase letters

a _____ b _____ c _____ d _____

e _____ f _____ g _____ h _____

i _____ j _____ k _____ l _____

m _____ n _____ o _____ p _____

q _____ r _____ s _____ t _____

u _____ v _____ w _____ x _____

y _____ z _____

MISSING LETTERS

Fill in the missing letter in the first box in each row. Then write a **rhyming word** in the second box and draw a picture of it.

_en	_en
_ut	_ut
_og	_og

abcdefghijklmnopqrstuvwxyz

MISSING LETTERS

Fill in the missing letter in the first box in each row. Then write a **rhyming word** in the second box and draw a picture of it.

abcdefghijklmnopqrstuvwxyz

MISSING LETTERS

Help the worm reach the apple by writing the missing letters.

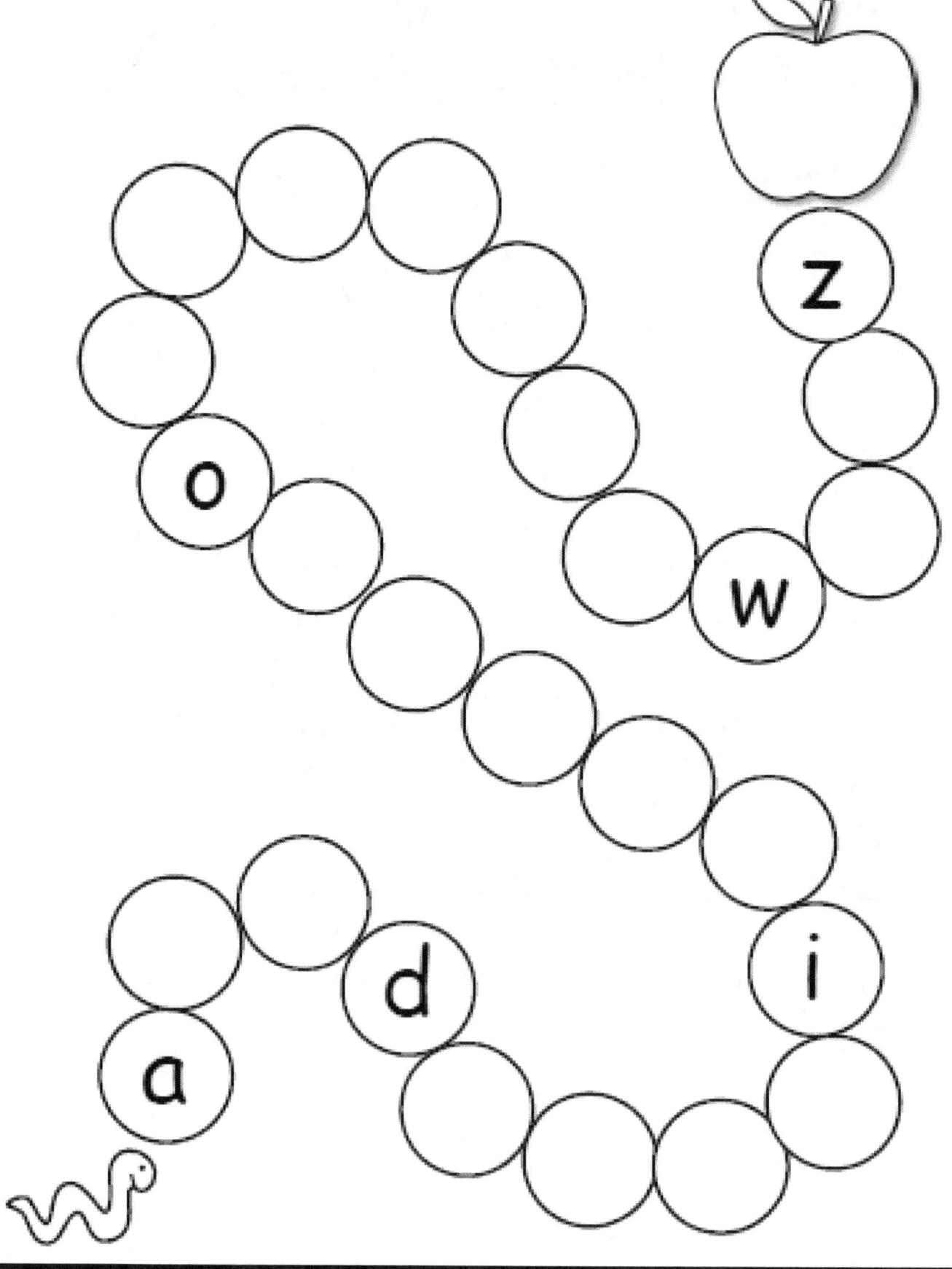

MATCHING LETTERS

Math the uppercase letter to the lowercase letter.

A	k
D	f
K	p
F	a
P	d

U	w
I	f
K	u
W	q
Q	i

Y	n
B	e
E	c
N	b
C	y

J	t
H	e
M	j
T	h
Z	m

DOT READING

Point to each dot as an adult says the word. When you get to a picture, it's your turn to read!

The  loved  . He wanted to

eat it before the  . The

was hungry for the  and the  .

Could the  eat both ?

STORY TIME

Complete the story by filling in the missing letters. The picture clues will help you.

One day the s__n was shining. The d__g was sleeping. The c__t was sleeping. But the h__n saw a f__x.

"Help! Help!" she cried.

The __at and the __og hid in a b__n. The __en flew into a h__t. The fo__ jumped into a b__ __, and the __ __n

went on shining.

www.ingramcontent.com/pod-product-compliance
Lightning Source LLC
LaVergne TN
LVHW060203080526
838202LV00052B/4193